The Zen of Photography

How to Take Pictures With Your Mind's Camera

Paul Martin Lester, Ph.D.

Writers Club Press

San Jose New York Lincoln Shanghai

The Zen of Photography
How to Take Pictures With Your Mind's Camera

Published by Writers Club Press
an imprint of iUniverse.com, Inc.

For information address:
iUniverse.com, Inc.
620 North 48th Street
Suite 201
Lincoln, NE 68504-3467
www.iuniverse.com

ISBN: 0-595-09782-0

Printed in the United States of America

For Allison and Denison,
the two suns in my life.

Introduction

I understand that my message will only be heard by those who are ready to listen and those who already know.

For those who do not listen and will not know, read on with an open heart.

1

It is said that every journey begins with a first step. Strive to make your first step a humble one.

2

Your real goal is not to learn photography but to learn how to live your life.

3

The goal is not to change your subjects, but for the subject to change the photographer.

4

When you use a camera, not as a machine but as an extension of your heart, you become one with your subject.

5

The type of photographs you make, the subjects you single out, reveal the person inside of you. How close you get to your subjects reveals how close you want to get.

6

Don't ever forget how alien a machine over a person's face appears. A photographer must be sensitive and caring so the mechanical act of recording light images is secondary to the union of spirit with the subject.

7

Don't use photography as an excuse to separate yourself from what you sense. You are what you see and feel. Don't be afraid to see with feeling.

8

It is best that a photographer not simply take a picture. A photographer has a responsibility to share a visual experience with others by every possible means.

9

A photographer becomes one with the world. Instead of making a photograph, the experience makes the photographer.

10

A teacher learns from the students. Who then is the real teacher/student? If the teacher is the student, then we are all students learning from each other.

11

Don't be afraid to be a little crazy. One definition of crazy: distracted with desire or excitement. Yes, I am crazy.

12

Don't ever get too serious about what you do. Life is full of joy. Laughter is an outward sign of that joy. Show me a friend who has a genuine, spontaneous laugh and you've shown me a person who is close to the truth.

13

Be flexible. Be open to every idea. They are all one idea. Your idea.

14

A tear contains an ocean. A photographer is aware of the tiny moments in a person's life that reveal greater truths.

15

Rules bind the soul. They are for the intellect.
A loving heart has no need of rules.

16

Life is not complicated. The mind makes life complex. The heart shows the mind that life is simple. Silence your mind and hear your heart.

17

It is useless to try to seek the truth. One day, the truth will seek you. When you climb a mountain and reach the crest, you look below and long for level ground. When you are not looking, then you will see.

18

We are all on different schedules. Readiness between individuals is a rare and beautiful event.

19

We all have our own path. We can all learn from our path through gentle faith.

20

A photographer strives to be fully aware of every moment and to be one with all others every moment.

21

If you can find pleasure and laugh at a flat tire on a lonely country road during a late night thunderstorm, you are close.

22

Any gift that comes from the heart goes to the heart.

23

What is supposed to happen to you is happening. Sit back, relax and enjoy. It is that simple. It is that difficult.

24

If God is loving, how can there be so much suffering? If you are loving, how can you not embrace suffering?

25

There is no difference between you and me, far and near, then and now. Enlightenment is a lover's song or a taxi's horn, a mountain peak or a polluted creek, a distant memory or reading these words.

26

Since no one can learn unless ready, the best teacher does not give answers. The best teacher facilitates questions.

27

Be a real student and take chances. Live on the edge. Teeter on the brink. Skip on the tightrope. And if you fall, enjoy the wind on your smiling face.

28

Develop through practice the energy for being aware. Satori moments are always happening.

29

Even at the risk of looking foolish and of persons shaking their heads and whispering that you must be crazy, try new things.

30

You are the creator of your universe. What you see is an illusion meant to teach you.

31

Seek out and learn from those who are different. Those who dress colorfully, those who dance to recorded music while waiting in a grocery store's check-out lane, or those who eat their dessert first. But remember: the more you know about people, the more you realize that we are all different.

32

Now is all there is. And it is because of what has happened to you before.

33

Change is natural. Adaptation to change is also natural. Don't be afraid of change.

34

Make all your choices with your heart, not your mind. Once a decision is made, use your mind to get to that place.

35

We are all one. You learn from all experiences—the good and the bad ones. Once you learn that lesson, there are no bad experiences, really.

36

Develop the confidence to never be afraid to be yourself.

37

Watch out for ego. It is always in the way. If someone says, "You have nice eyes." Reply, "Thank you. They do the job."

38

Truth is what works for you. It is no one else's truth but your truth.

39

"Why were you late?" "Karma is karma."

40

I am every thought, every feeling and every vision I have ever experienced.

41

A total person has equal parts of feminine and masculine traits. A whole person is able to say, "I am woman/man enough to let my feminine/masculine qualities show."

42

Answers from the heart are always simple. It is our mind that makes the answer complex.

43

Life is your art. An open, aware heart is your camera. A oneness with your world is your film. Your bright eyes and easy smile is your museum.

44

Ask yourself, "Why am I seeing and feeling this? How am I growing? What am I learning?" Remember: Every coincidence is potentially meaningful. How high your awareness level is determines how much meaning you get from your world. Photography can teach you to improve your awareness level.

45

Look at the ruts you've fallen in. Do something about changing them. Be in touch with your feeling so you will spontaneously know when and how to change. Don't think too much about it. We use our minds too much as it is.

46

What is the ultimate reality? Being fully aware of this and every moment.

47

A photographer does not operate a camera in order to merely take pictures. Photographic work is always personal. A photograph reveals the photographer.

48

By knowing a person, you know yourself. You become the person you photograph. You love that person as you love yourself.

49

Unless you experience, you cannot really know.

50

Through constant practice you will become so skilled technically that you will no longer need to think consciously of the camera's operation. At that point you will break the machine wall between you and the person photographed.

51

The type of camera you use for photography makes no difference. A loving, open heart makes a photograph, not a camera.

52

Do not concern yourself with the questions, "What is art?" or "Who is an artist?" Everything is art. If what you see and do comes from your heart, you are an artist.

53

Everyone is special. Everyone has something to say and to give. Any person becomes creative when you know yourself and can release that energy that is uniquely yours.

54

When you experience something, you learn from it. By learning from it you know that you are like it and it is like you. Once you discover that connection, you love it as you love yourself. The oneness is complete through the energy of love. This lesson can be learned from a flower, a kitten or a cross-country truck driver.

55

You do not think of your feet when you walk. Likewise, become so accustomed to your camera that its function becomes an extension of yourself.

56

Children know how to be natural. Only a child can walk into an empty shopping mall, yell at the silence and play with the sound of the echo. How old is a child? At what age does the child die? When a person ceases to act naturally, the child dies.

57

Spontaneity is an instantaneous decision from the heart.

58

Do not see with just your eyes. If so, you are simply turning yourself into another machine. See with your heart and not with your eyes.

59

There is no need to hurry for there is no goal to run towards. The goal is with you already. You'll miss your goal if you hurry.

60

Because we let our machines see for us, we forget how to feel. A machine is never moved by a sunset; a heart is.

61

By seeing things in terms of what they are used for, the real meaning is lost. A bicycle is a vehicle. Deeper—it is a noise. Deeper still—it is yourself.

62

Because we have forgotten to look with our hearts, we see objects and we make persons into objects that we either use or avoid. We have the opportunity to make every chance meeting significant if we have the energy necessary for that appreciation.

63

The energy needed to be constantly aware comes from love.

64

You need not photograph a thing to know it. All you need to do is spend time with your full concentration with the thing, person or emotion. One way instead of On way. Another way is by opening your heart.

65

The past is a learning memory. The future is a yearning goal. The present is the only moment that exists. You can stretch that moment out forever if you are constantly aware of every now.

66

No camera, pen or sheet of paper is needed to feel one with your world. But it is a funny thing. Once you feel the world's connection with yourself, you find an outlet for expressing that connection. It may be in photography, poetry, painting, volunteering in a nursing home, or simply by your bright eyes and smile. You'll find it.

67

The photographic process is so simple. A gorilla took a picture used on a National Geographic cover. There is a danger in that photography is so easy. The taking is easy. The feeling is difficult.

68

I was looking for a teacher and I found myself.

69

Your equipment does not matter as long as you are comfortable with it. Comfortable is an important word. It is the opposite of self-conscious.

70

You must know yourself and your subject well before you can take a picture. You must become one with it.

71

Every person has a story to tell. Every person is looking for a caring spirit that will listen.

72

When you know another person as yourself, you learn from that person. When you feel, all persons are your teachers.

73

A photograph is just a picture if it doesn't say anything.

74

The mind makes pictures. The heart makes photographs.

75

When you begin to care you realize, as you look in a passersby eyes, we have all experienced the same tragedies, triumphs and fits of boredom. We all feel the same emotions. We are all the same person.

76

We are put on the earth to love and learn.

77

Learning is not an end. It is an endless process.

78

It is not enough to be a good photographer. You also need to be a good person who takes pictures.

79

Anything can be practiced. A guitar piece to a positive way of life. Practice is simply concentrating on a single action or idea until it no longer exists in your conscious mind.

80

A snapshot, like a sketch, is a quickly composed image. Both can be important if both communicate the artist's feelings about the subject.

81

You can only learn when you are ready to listen.

82

Cave drawings reveal a seeing not hindered by words.

83

Feeling must be the end result—not a drawing, not a painting, and not a photograph. It is what you learn from an experience that is important not whether you have something to show.

84

A shutter only clicks quickly after a sensitive heart has felt the subject a long time.

85

Let your mind make the technical decisions.
Let your heart make the content decisions.

86

Once you learn to care, you can record images with your mind or on film. There is no difference between the two.

87

That which matters most is more than f-stops and lenses, more than pens and papers, more than notes and strings, more than knives and clay. That which matters most is a child's laugh, a lover's hug, an open heart.

88

Technology interferes with the spirit. Machinery suppresses the fun. The mind thwarts the heart.

89

Another word for prana or absolute energy is love.

90

Through photography you learn that all persons are teachers.

91

A strong ego prevents you from asking questions. Don't be afraid to look silly. Don't be afraid to learn from anyone.

92

The truth is in all things. Weston found truth in a bed pan.

93

Your goal is not to be the best photographer, the best runner, the best musician, the best writer, or the best anything. Your goal, if you feel you really need a goal, is to be yourself.

94

There are three phases to awareness: to look, to see, and to perceive. A camera looks. A mind sees. A heart perceives.

95

Art is a way of living, of caring, of giving, of loving.

96

You cannot want to be anything. Either you are or you are not. If you are, you are being your natural self and peace will come. If you are not, your ego directs your actions and you will always be disturbed.

97

You can only teach when you are ready to listen.

98

Love is the bottom line. Love is the energy in all things. When you feel for another, when you get close to another, you love that person.

99

Love cannot be diluted or diminished. It is only how we express love that gives love its various forms.

100

A camera is a hollow tube that allows free-flowing, inward and outward expressions of love between a photographer and a subject.

Epilogue

On the first day of my photojournalism class, I ask my students to give me a number from one to 100 when I call their name. A couple of them ask why, but I don't tell them. I record these numbers next to their name on the roll sheet. For the mid-term exam, they are asked to bring a 16-page blue book. I pass out the saying that corresponds with the number they gave me during the first day and tell them to write at least five pages on whatever comes to mind. They can also include photographs, drawings, poetry, and so on. I am amazed at the depth of their responses. I receive many of their favorite pictures, stories of why they love photography, and personal revelations included in their blue books. I've come to the conclusion that we all long for a way to express ourselves emotionally—something we don't get to do too often. What follows are brief excerpts from each student.

Everything I take a picture of, I try to think of it as a new invention for someone to see. If it comes out perfect it is because I put my heart into it. And if the viewer likes it, it is because his or her heart and emotions accepted it.

The quote I was given has nothing to do with photography knowledge, the quote is dealing with life knowledge, everything else falls into place.

There is so much to be thankful for. For beautiful sunsets. For the way dew glistens on spider webs. For the early morning, when there is peace, and the birds softly talk to one another. For moments when you feel the world stops and you have that moment etched into your mind forever. For the smile and laugh from a dear friend. For a special glance from that special love in your life. For the way cats curl up and cause you to sit there peacefully and pet them until they have had enough. For a child's laugh. For a good song. For a touching photograph. For the moments these things last, they seem to bring such great happiness.

They somehow bring you into the place you wish you were always, aware of every moment. Living for the now, not the future not the past.

I think a photography class should be a requirement in all educational programs because it makes you see the world rather than just look at it. And by seeing we also begin to understand ourselves.

When we care, we will not forget. The picture in our head or the vivid printed picture will remind us. Without care, we would not remember, only see.

My camera has helped to give me insight to truth. It has helped me to understand that change is wonderful and beneficial.

Pictures always should have a special story behind it or a special meaning to the photographer.

Pictures hold life's experiences. And I feel that with every experience you learn something. Therefore, you learn something with every picture you take.

I've noticed in my photography that I do a lot better when I'm on vacation. I'm more relaxed and true to my own senses. I really think that's the only route to pure happiness.

I enjoy photography, that's why I do it. If you are taking pictures you are not enjoying, don't take them. If you are stuck behind the camera and would rather stop taking pictures and play; go play.

I think that when the subject allows the photographer to accompany him/her and witness all his/her private moments, the photographer should give something in return. I see it like a contract where the photographer has to pay the price for being allowed the life of the subject.

This is how I live my life and keep myself a happy person and a good photographer-I take in everything around me and live every moment as if it could be the last.

We show our love by our deeds.

Photography is a very special art. It is the only place in the world that I know in which time can be stopped in a single moment, frozen in one moment. Years and years after that moment passes by, you can still see and feel the moment in the images that are captured. You can still learn and understand the truth of a single moment in the lives of the people or events in the pictures you view.

We are all sensitive human beings. Just because we are photographers doesn't mean we should forget this. Each and every person we have contact with in our lives on any occasion, is an opportunity to join our spirits with theirs. If a photograph can represent the union of spirits, then a photographer has succeeded not only in their job, but also in one of the most beautiful experiences in life.

We are living in the world which continuously flows and never stops or goes back. Even in a 24-hour day, people might have hundreds of facial expressions, not only anger, happiness, anxiety or sadness, sometimes more complex emotions show up on their faces. I will see them every moment, but since they are continuously changing, the moments of various expressions might not remain in my memory so powerful as they did. I hope I will be able to do this with my camera.

I really think that a good balance between mind and heart is what makes a healthy person. The more you strive to be equal, the more you'll take life in stride and not be so stressed out all the time.

This saying is pretty timely. With some animosity, I jumped into the project with both feet. Hoping for the best, I made dozens of phone calls to several different shelters and organizations. As time rolled on and nobody was returning my calls, I was getting restless and annoyed. Now as I take a look back at the whole project, I understand more about homelessness. More importantly though, I learned a lot about myself. I learned how to be more open and talk to strangers. But I also learned a lot about flexibility.

Trying something for the first time can be nerve racking as well as exciting. I was able to take some kids to the beach for the first time and I was amazed at how crazy they got. One moment they were normal children and the next thing I knew they were running around the sand amazed at how cool it was and how exciting seeing the ocean for the first time really is.

Each photograph you take teaches you something about yourself and about life and the world in general. I am not making the photograph, the image is already there waiting to be discovered and captured. In discovering emotionally moving scenes and images, we are learning something new about ourselves and the subject involved. Every experience builds upon another to help form who you are.

Spontaneity is what makes life worth living. It leads to change, which in turn leads to growth and fulfillment. Complacency leads to stagnation and decline. Humans are goal-oriented creatures. We must always be striving for something in order to have purpose and a sense of peace. Through struggle, contentment. The End is not what matters, at least not while we're "alive." The means, the journey, the experience—that's where the adventure lies.

For me, my camera is my eye and my brain is the film that keeps those images recorded. But there is something in me that the camera does not have and it is the heart. When I see images in my mind, I feel the emotions in my heart and they are what I mean by saying that it is something that the camera does not have. The camera can capture the image, just as I can, but the camera cannot feel what I feel.

About the Author

Paul Martin Lester is a Professor of Communications at California State University, Fullerton. After an undergraduate degree in journalism from the University of Texas at Austin and employment as a photo-journalist for *The Times-Picayune* in New Orleans, Lester received a Master's from the University of Minnesota and a Ph.D. from Indiana University in mass communications. He is the author or editor of seven books: *Visual Communication Images with Messages Second Edition, Images that Injure Pictorial Stereotypes in the Media, Desktop Computing Workbook, Photojournalism An Ethical Approach, The Ethics of Photojournalism, The Spiral Web On the Nature of Coincidence, and The Zen of Photography.*